Songbook

Authors

Lynn M. Brinckmeyer Texas State University, San Marcos, Texas

Amy M. Burns Far Hills Country Day School, Far Hills, New Jersey

Patricia Shehan Campbell University of Washington, Seattle, Washington

Audrey Cardany University of Rhode Island, Kingston, Rhode Island

Shelly Cooper University of Nebraska at Omaha, Omaha, Nebraska

Anne M. Fennell Vista Unified School District, Vista, California

Sanna Longden Clinician/Consultant, Evanston, Illinois

Rochelle G. Mann Fort Lewis College, Durango, Colorado

Nan L. McDonald San Diego State University, San Diego, California

Martina Miranda University of Colorado, Boulder, Colorado

Sandra L. Stauffer Arizona State University, Tempe, Arizona

Phyllis Thomas Lewisville Independent School District, Lewisville, Texas

Charles Tighe Cobb County School District, Atlanta, Georgia

Maribeth Yoder-White Clinician/Consultant, Banner Elk, North Carolina

 in partnership with

Boston, Massachusetts
Chandler, Arizona
Glenview, Illinois
New York, New York

interactive MUSIC powered by Silver Burdett™ with Alfred Music Publishing Co., Inc.

PEARSON

ISBN-13: 978-1-4182-6267-9
ISBN-10:   1-4182-6267-6
11 19

Abiyoyo

Bantu Lullaby

A - bi - yo - yo, _____ a - bi - yo - yo, _____

A - bi - yo - yo, _____ a - bi - yo - yo; _____

A - bi - yo - yo, bi - yo - yo, bi - yo - yo, _____

A - bi - yo - yo, bi - yo - yo, bi - yo - yo. _____

Achshav
(Awake! Awake!)

Folk Song from Israel
English Words by David Eddleman

Ach - shav, ach - shav, b' - em - ek Yis - ra - el;
A - wake! A - wake! the val - leys of our land,

Ach - shav, ach - shav, b' - em - ek Yis - ra - el.
A - wake! A - wake! the val - leys of our land.

Tum - ba, tum - ba, tum - ba, b' - em - ek Yis - ra - el, Hey!
Tum - ba, tum - ba, tum - ba, the land of Is - ra - el, Hey!

Tum - ba, tum - ba, tum - ba, b' - em - ek Yis - ra - el, Hey!
Tum - ba, tum - ba, tum - ba, the land of Is - ra - el, Hey!

Al ánimo

Folk Song from Spain
English Words by Alice Firgau

Allegro

VERSE

do—

1. Al   á - ni-mo, al   á - ni-mo, la   fuen-te   se   rom-pió,
2. Al   á - ni-mo, al   á - ni-mo, ¿con   qué se ha-ce el   di - nero?
1. Al   á - ni-mo, al   á - ni-mo, The   foun-tain has gone   dry.
2. Al   á - ni-mo, al   á - ni-mo, From   what   is   mon-ey   made?

Al   á - ni-mo, al   á - ni-mo, man - dar-la a com-po - ner.
Al   á - ni-mo, al   á - ni-mo, con   cás - ca - ra   de   huevo.
Al   á - ni-mo, al   á - ni-mo, Then   fix   it   do   not   cry.
Al   á - ni-mo, al   á - ni-mo, From   cot - ton thread and   braid.

REFRAIN

¡Hu - rí, hu - rí, hu - rá!   La   rei - na va a pa - sar,
Hu - rí, hu - rí, hu - rá!   The   queen is pass - ing   by,

¡Hu - rí, hu - rí, hu - rá!   La   rei - na va a pa - sar.
Hu - rí, hu - rí, hu - rá!   The   queen is pass - ing   by.

3

America

Traditional Melody ("God Save the King")
Words by Samuel Francis Smith

Au clair de la lune
(In the Moonlight)

Traditional Song from France
English Version by D. Auberge

Au clair de la lu - ne, Mon a - mi Pier - rot,
Stand - ing in the moon - light, Mon a - mi Pier - rot,

Prê - te - moi ta plu - me, Pour é - crire un mot;
I have lost my can - dle, How, I do not know!

Ma chan - delle est mor - te, je n'ai plus de feu.
If you can - not help me, I will have to stay

Ou - vre - moi ta por - te, Pour l'a - mour de Dieu.
Stand - ing in the dark - ness, 'til the light of day.

B-A, Bay

Folk Song from the United States

A

F   C7

B - A, bay,   B - E, bee,   B - I, bid-die by,   B - O, bo,

C7   F

Bid - die by bo, B - U, bu, bid-die by bo bu, bu.

B

Bb   F

This is just a sil - ly song! The words don't mean a thing.

Dm   Bb   C7

Nev - er mind the sil - ly words, Just o - pen up and sing. Oh!

F   C7

B - A, bay,   B - E, bee,   B - I, bid-die by,   B - O, bo,

C7   F

Bid - die by bo, B - U, bu, bid-die by bo bu, bu.

HACKETT, PATRICIA, MELODY BOOK, THE: 300 SELECTIONS FROM THE WORLD OF MUSIC FOR PIANO,
GUITAR, AUTOHARP, RECORDER AND VOICE, 3rd Ed., ©1998.
Reprinted and Electronically reproduced by permission of Pearson Education, Inc., Upper Saddle River, New Jersey.

Banjo Sam

Folk Song from North Carolina

VERSE

1. Cat - fish, cat - fish, go - in' up - stream,
2. As I was go - in' through the field,
3. As I was go - in' down___ the road,

A Cat - fish, cat - fish where you been?
black___ snake bit me on the heel.
I met___ a ter - ra - pin and a toad.

I grabbed that cat - fish by___ the snout,
I grabbed a stick and done___ my best,
The ter - ra - pin, he be - gan___ to sing,

I pulled___ that cat - fish wrong - side out.
And ran___ my head in a hor - net's nest.
The toad,___ he cut the pi - geon - wing.

REFRAIN

Yo - ho!_____ Ban - jo Sam!

7

Bob-a-Needle

African American Ring Game

Bob - a - need - le, bob - a - need - le is a - run - ning.

Bob - a - need - le, bob - a - need - le is a run - ning,

Bet - ter hide, bob - a - need - le, bob - a - need - le is a run - ning,

Bet - ter hus - tle, bob - a - need - le, bob - a - need - le is a run - ning,

I'll catch bob - a - need - le, bob - a - need - le's not a run - ning.

Canoe Song

Words and Music by Margaret E. McGhee

1. My pad - dle's keen and bright, Flash - ing with sil - ver,
2. Dip, dip and swing her back, Flash - ing with sil - ver,

Fol - low the wild goose flight, Dip, dip and swing.
Fol - low the wild goose track, Dip, dip and swing.

Che che koolay

Folk Song from Ghana

Chicka Hanka

African American Work Song

Chrismus a Come

Traditional Song from Jamaica

do

Chris - mus a come, me wan___ me la - ma,

Chris - mus a come, me wan___ me la - ma,

Chris - mus a come, me wan___ me deg - ge - day,

Chris - mus a come, me wan___ me deg - ge - day.

Cookie

Calypso Song from the West Indies

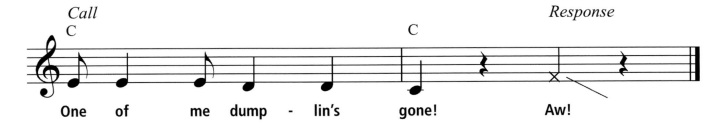

The Crocodile

Traditional

do

She sailed a - way on a love - ly sum - mer day

on the back of a croc - o - dile;

"You'll see," said she, "he's as tame as tame can be,

I'll ride him down the Nile."

The Crocodile

The croc winked his eye as she bade them all good-bye,

wear- ing a hap - py smile;

At the end of the ride the lad - y was in - side

and the smile was on the croc - o - dile!

(Spoken)

dile! Yum Yum!

Dinah

Folk Song from the United States

No one's in the house but Di - nah, Di - nah,

No one's in the house but me, I know.

No one's in the house but Di - nah, Di - nah,

Strum - min' on the old ban - jo.

Down, Down, Baby

African American Clapping Song

Down, Down, Baby

P - O - P spells POP!

2.
Grand - ma, Grand - ma - ma, sick in bed,

Called the doc - tor and the doc - tor said,_____

N.C.
"Let's get the mo - tion of the head, ding dong,

Let's get the mot - ion of the hands, clap clap,

Let's get the mo - tion of the feet, stomp stomp

Down, Down, Baby

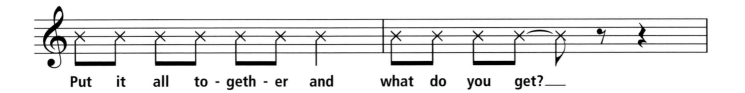

Put it all to - geth - er and what do you get? ___

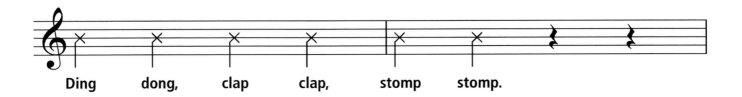

Ding dong, clap clap, stomp stomp.

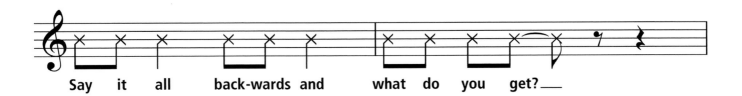

Say it all back-wards and what do you get? ___

Stomp stomp, clap clap, ding dong!"

Down in the Valley Two by Two

Folk Song
Arranged by Robert W. Smith

Down in the Valley Two by Two

Let me see you make a mo - tion, ___ two by two, ___

now ___ rise, Sal - ly, rise. ___

VERSE

3. Let me see you make an - o - ther one, ___ two by two, ___ my ba - by,

two by two, ___ my ba - by, two by two. ___

Let me see you make an - o - ther one, ___ two by two, ___

now ___ rise, Sal - ly, rise. ___

Down in the Valley Two by Two

4. Now   choose some - bod - y,   two   by   two,___   my   ba - by,

two   by   two,___   my   ba - by,   two   by   two.___

Choose_   some - bod - y,   two   by   two,___

now_   rise,   Sal - ly   rise.___   Go!

Down in the Valley Two by Two

Percussion

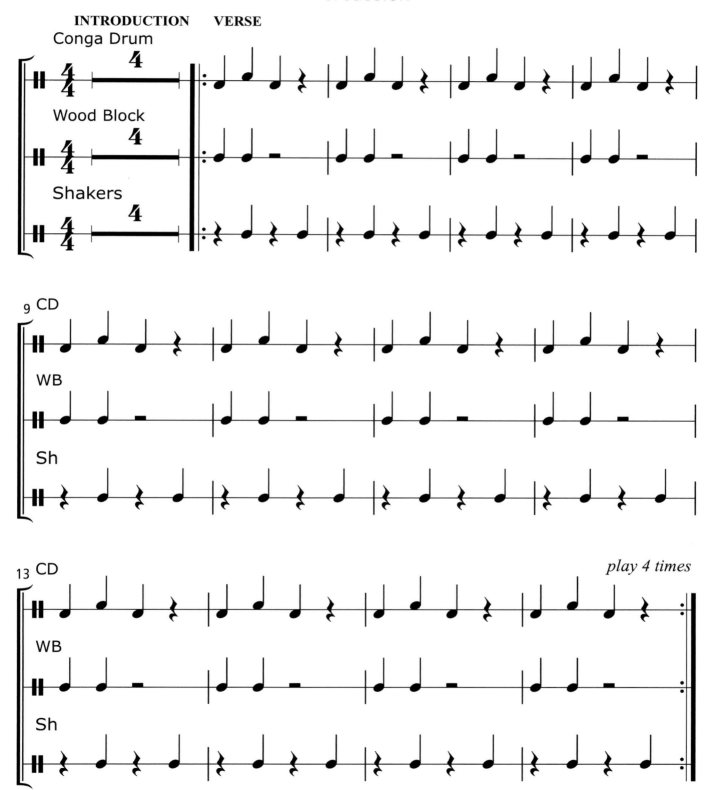

Down the Ohio

River Shanty

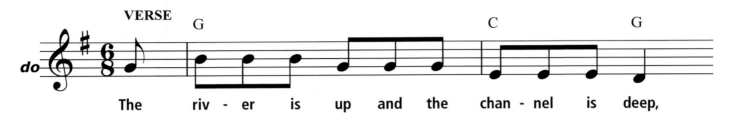

do **VERSE** G ... C ... G

The riv - er is up and the chan - nel is deep,

D7 ... G ... D7

The wind is stead - y and strong.

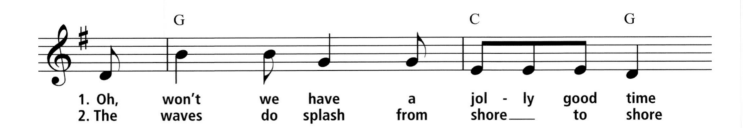

G ... C ... G

1. Oh, won't we have a jol - ly good time
2. The waves do splash from shore___ to shore

D7 ... G

As we go sail - ing a - long.

Down the Ohio

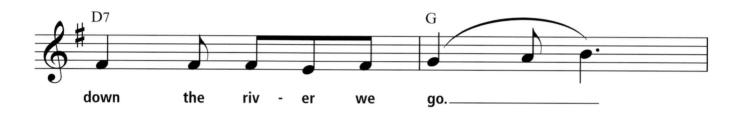

Dr. Seuss, We Love You

Words and Music by Carmino Ravosa

REFRAIN

Doc-tor Seuss, we love you, Doc-tor Seuss, we real-ly do,

Doc-tor Seuss, we love_____ you.

Fine

VERSE

1. With your rhymes so cra-zy, You are num-ber one.
2. We like *Yer-tle the Tur-tle,* We like *Sam I Am.*

D.C. al Fine

Make us laugh and won-der, You make read-ing fun.
Like the *Grinch* and *Lor-ax,* and *Green Eggs and Ham.*

Earthworm, Earthworm

Words and Music by
Sally K. Albrecht and Jay Althouse

Earthworm, Earthworm

Working your way through hard and rocky ground.

Providing air to plants at their roots,

helping them to bear much richer fruits.

Earthworm, earthworm, secretly you make me squirm,

but you are more important than we think.

Ecologic'ly you're one important link.

Ecologic'ly you're one important link.

El barquito
(The Tiny Boat)

Folk Song from Latin America
English Words by Kim Williams

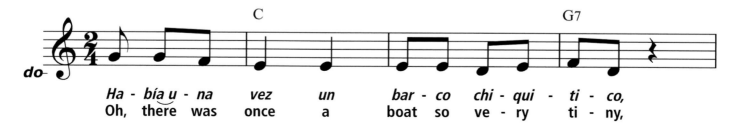

Ha - bía u - na vez un bar - co chi - qui - ti - co,
Oh, there was once a boat so ve - ry ti - ny,

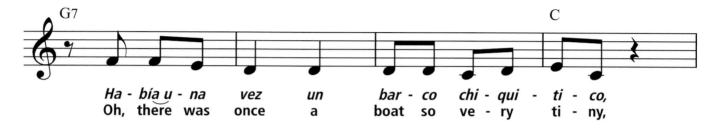

Ha - bía u - na vez un bar - co chi - qui - ti - co,
Oh, there was once a boat so ve - ry ti - ny,

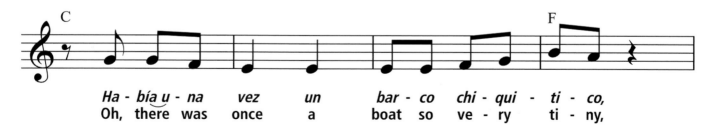

Ha - bía u - na vez un bar - co chi - qui - ti - co,
Oh, there was once a boat so ve - ry ti - ny,

Que no po - dí - a, que no po - dí - a, que no po -
So ve - ry tin - y, so ve - ry ti - ny, it could not

dí - a na - ve - gar. Pa - sa - ron u - na, dos, tres,
e - ven sail a - way. It sat for one, two, three, four,

El barquito

cua - tro, cin - co, seis, sie - te se - ma - nas.
five, six, sev - en weeks there in the har - bor.

Pa - sa - ron u - na, dos, tres, cua - tro, cin - co,
It sat for one, two, three, four, five, six, sev - en

seis, sie - te se - ma - nas. Pa - sa - ron
weeks there in the har - bor. It sat for

u - na, dos, tres, cua - tro, cin - co, seis, sie - te se -
one, two, three, four, five, six, sev - en weeks there in the

ma - nas. Y el bar - qui - to, que no po -
har - bor. It was so ti - ny, so ve - ry

dí - a, que no po - dí - a na - ve - gar.
ti - ny, It could not e - ven sail a - way.

El florón
(The Flower)

Singing Game from Puerto Rico
English Words by Verne Muñoz

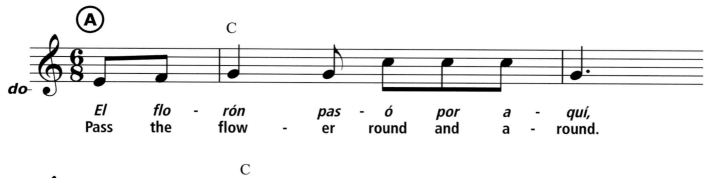

El flo - rón pas - ó por a - quí,
Pass the flow - er round and a - round.

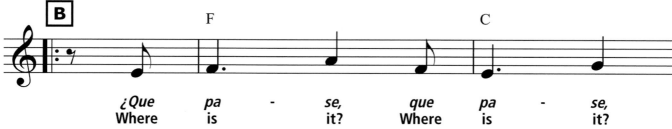

Yo no lo vi, Yo no lo vi.
Will it be found? Will it be found?

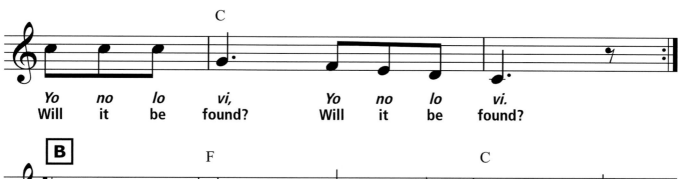

¿Que pa - se, que pa - se,
Where is it? Where is it?

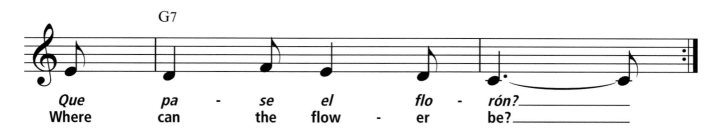

Que pa - se el flo - rón?_____
Where can the flow - er be?_____

31

El tambor
(The Drum)

Folk Song from Mexico

Every Morning When I Wake Up

Words and Music by Avon Gillespie

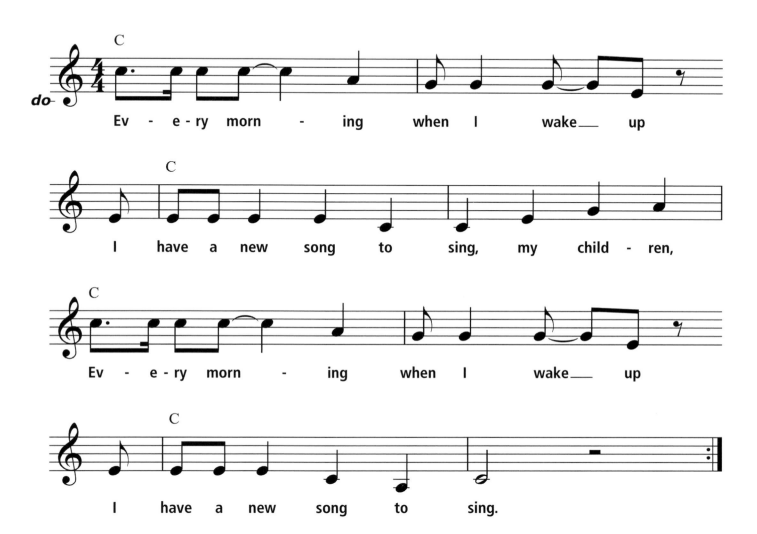

Ev'rybody Smiles in the Same Language

Words and Music by Carmino Ravosa

Ev - 'ry - bod - y smiles in the same lan - guage,

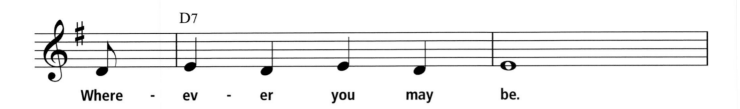

Where - ev - er you may be.

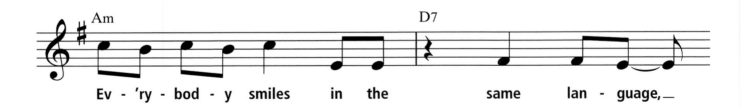

Ev - 'ry - bod - y smiles in the same lan - guage,

just look and you will see.

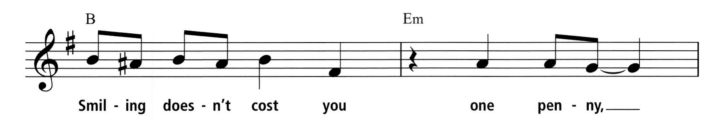

Smil - ing does - n't cost you one pen - ny,

"Ev'rybody Smiles in the Same Language" © 1995 Silver Burdett Ginn

Ev'rybody Smiles in the Same Language

You can give 'em free, 'cause you got so man - y.

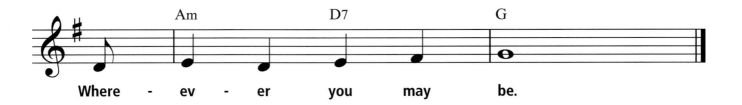

Ev - 'ry - bod - y smiles in the same lan - guage,—

Where - ev - er you may be.

Four in a Boat

Play-Party Song from Appalachia

1. Four in a boat and the tide rolls high,
2. Choose your part - ner and stay all day,
3. Eight in a boat and it won't go 'round,

Four in a boat and the tide rolls high,
Choose your part - ner and stay all day,
Eight in a boat and it won't go 'round,

Four in a boat and the tide rolls high,
Choose your part - ner and stay all day,
Eight in a boat and it won't go 'round,

Wait-ing for a pret - ty one to come bye and bye.
We don't care what the old folks say.
Swing that pret - ty one that you just found.

Four in a Boat

Rhythm: Reading ♫, ♩, and 𝄾

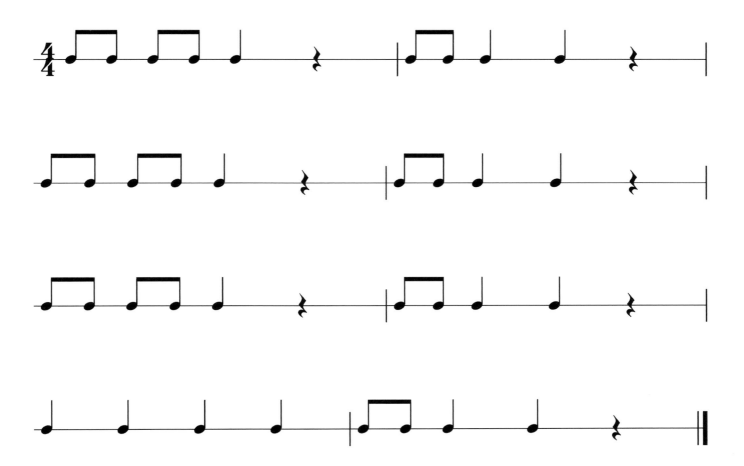

Frère Jacques
(Are You Sleeping?)

Folk Song from France

Frè - re Jac - ques, Frè - re Jac - ques,
Are you sleep - ing, Are you sleep - ing,

Dor - mez vous?_____ Dor - mez vous?_____
Broth - er John?_____ Broth - er John?_____

Son - nez les ma - ti - nes, Son - nez les ma - ti - nes,
Morn - ing bells are ring - ing, Morn - ing bells are ring - ing,

Din, dan, don,_____ din, dan, don._____
ding, dang, dong,_____ ding dang, dong._____

Frog and Toad Together

Words and Music by Carmino Ravosa

1. Frog and Toad to - geth - er. They real - ly are a pair.
2. Frog and Toad to - geth - er. They have a lot of fun.
3. Frog and Toad to - geth - er. They're friends for - ev - er - more.

Last time To Coda

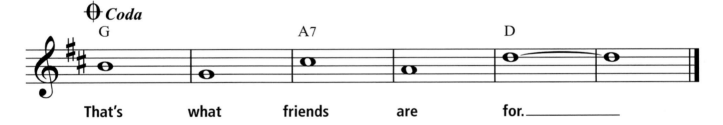

When you look for one of them, the oth - er will be there.
You'll al - ways find the two of them, you'll nev - er find just one.
Frog and toad to - geth - er, 'cause that's what friends are for.

Coda

That's what friends are for. _____

Goin' Over the Sea

Sea Shanty
Arranged by Michael Story

Goin' Over the Sea

Percussion

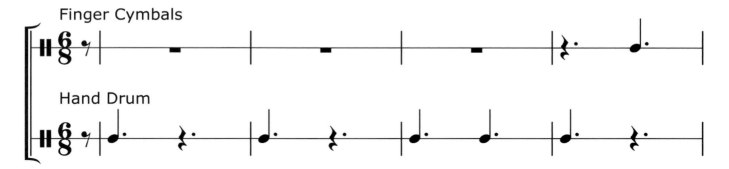

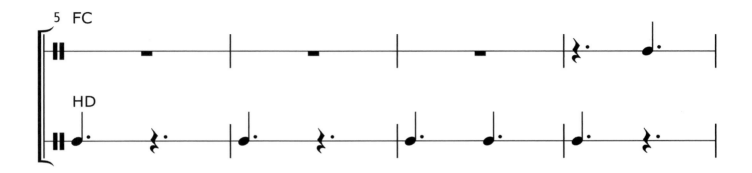

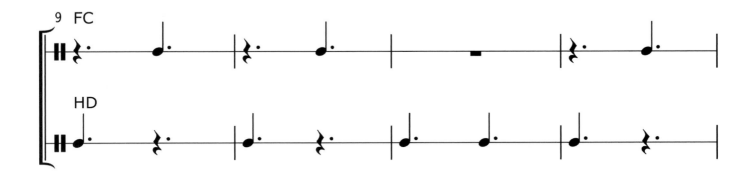

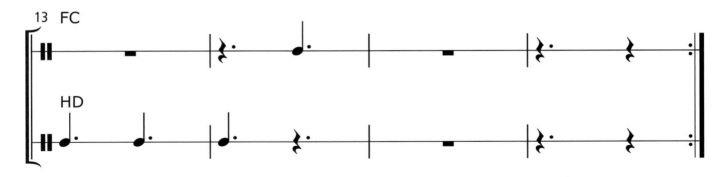

Great Big House

Play-Party Song from Louisiana

1. Great big house in New Or - leans,
2. Went down to the old mill stream to
3. Fare thee well, my dar - ling girl,

For - ty sto - ries high; _____
fetch a pail of wa - ter;
Fare thee well, my daugh - ter;

Ev - 'ry room that I've been in,
Put one arm a - round my wife, The
Fare thee well, my dar - ling girl, With

Filled with pump - kin pie.
oth - er 'round my daugh - ter.
gold - en slip - pers on her.

Great Big House

Melody: Reading a *do*-Pentatonic Song

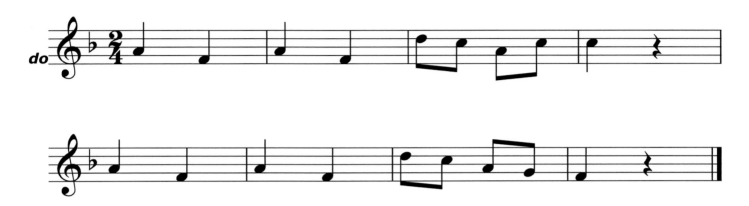

Haere

(Farewell)

Maori Song from New Zealand
Edited and Arranged by Patricia Sheehan Campbell,
Sue Williamson and Pierre Peron
English Words by David Eddleman

He's Got the Whole World in His Hands

African American Spiritual

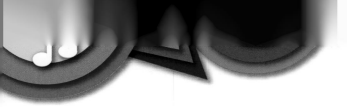

Hosisipa

Native American Game Song of the Sioux
By Louise Bradford

Ho - si - si - pa, ho - si - si - pa, ho - si - si - pa, ho - si.

How Many Miles to Babylon?

Game Song from England

How ma-ny miles to Ba - by - lon? Three score and ten.

Will we be there by can - dle - light? Yes, and back a - gain.

O - pen the gates and let us through. Not with - out a beck and bow.

Here's your beck; here's your bow! O - pen the gates and let us through.

I Fed My Horse

Folk Song from North Carolina

1. I fed my horse in a pop - lar trough,
   And there he caught the whoop - ing cough.
   I fed my horse in a pop - lar trough,
   And there he caught the whoop - ing cough.

2. I fed my horse in a sil - ver spoon,
   And then he kicked it over the moon.
   I fed my horse in a sil - ver spoon,
   And then he kicked it over the moon.

3. My old horse is dead and gone,
   But he left his jaw - bones ploughing the corn.
   My old horse is dead and gone,
   But he left his jaw - bones ploughing the corn.

CHOKSY, LOIS, KODALY CONTEXT, 1st Ed., ©1981, p. 246.
Reprinted and Electronically reproduced by permission of Pearson Education, Inc., Upper Saddle River, New Jersey.

I Fed My Horse

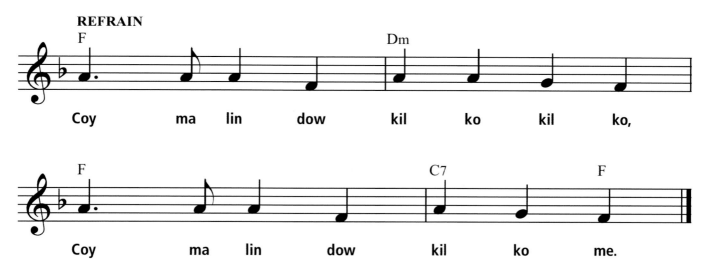

REFRAIN

Coy ma lin dow kil ko kil ko,

Coy ma lin dow kil ko me.

I'm on My Way

African American Spiritual

1. I'm on my way (I'm on my way) to the free-dom land, (to the free-dom
2. I asked my friends (I asked my friends) to___ go with me, (to___ go with
3. If they won't come (if they won't come) then I'll go a - lone, (then I'll go a -
4. I'm on my way (I'm on my way) and I won't turn back, (and I won't turn

land,) I'm on my way (I'm on my way) to the free-dom land, (to the free-dom
me,) I asked my friends (I asked my friends) to___ go with me, (to___ go with
lone,) If they won't come (if they won't come) then I'll go a - lone, (then I'll go a -
back,) I'm on my way (I'm on my way) and I won't turn back, (and I won't turn

land,) I'm on my way (I'm on my way) to the free-dom land, (to the free-dom
me,) I asked my friends (I asked my friends) to___ go with me, (to___ go with
lone,) If they won't come (if they won't come) then I'll go a - lone, (then I'll go a -
back,) I'm on my way (I'm on my way) and I won't turn back, (and I won't turn

land,)
me,)
lone,)   I'm on my way,___ thank God, I'm on my way._____
back,)

It's Santa–Again!

Words and Music by Elizabeth Gilpatrick

1. See the rein-deer tak-ing flight_____
2. Stashed be-hind him 'way in back_____

On a clear De-cem-ber night._____
I see his e-nor-mous pack._____

Can you see him flash-ing by,
I have heard it's filled with toys,

Out a-cross the win-ter sky?
For all the girls and all the boys.

You'll miss him if you blink your eye: it's San-ta a-gain!
Hush now, don't you make a noise: it's San-ta a-gain!

John Kanaka

Sea Shanty

Join the Conga Line

Words and Music by
Sally K. Albrecht and Jay Althouse

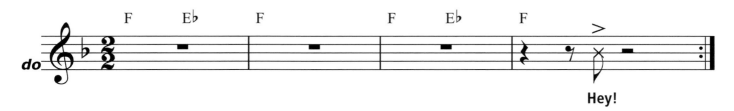

Hey!

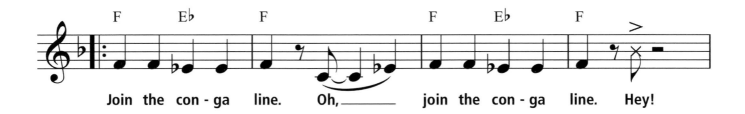

Join the con - ga line. Oh, _____ join the con - ga line. Hey!

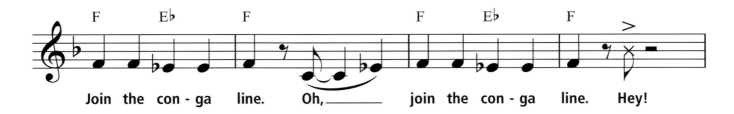

Join the con - ga line. Oh, _____ join the con - ga line. Hey!

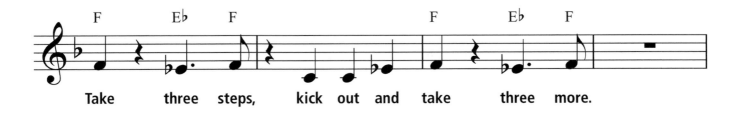

Take three steps, kick out and take three more.

Form a line, { and move a - round the floor. }
{ then dance right out the door. }

Join the Conga Line

Feel the ex - cite - ment. You'll want to shout for more. Ev - 'ry -

bod - y come. and join the con - ga line. Hey!

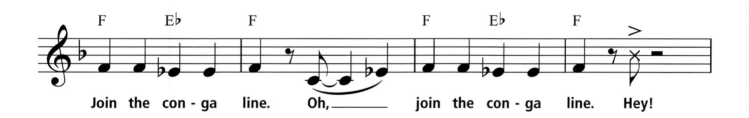

Join the con - ga line. Oh, _____ join the con - ga line. Hey!

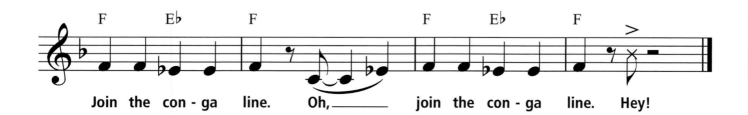

Join the con - ga line. Oh, _____ join the con - ga line. Hey!

Kapulu kane
(Puili Game Song)

Singing Game from Hawaii

Ka - pu - lu, pu - lu Ka - ne,   Ka - pu - lu, pu - lu Ka - ne,

Ka - pu - lu, pu - lu Ka - ne ku - ka - na - lu - a.

Ka - pu - lu, pu - lu Ka - ne,   Ka - pu - lu, pu - lu Ka - ne,

Ka - pu - lu, pu - lu Ka - ne ku - ka - na - lu - a.

Knock, Knock!

Words and Music by
Sally K. Albrecht and Jay Althouse

Knock, Knock!

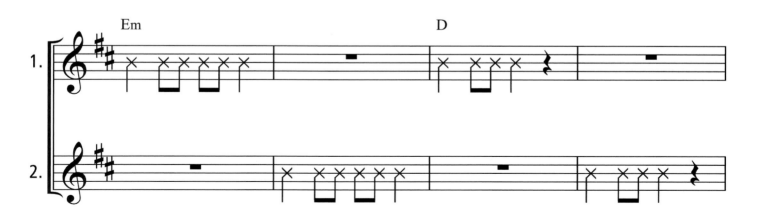

*Singers may knock their fist into their L palm. Or use a clipboard or other small piece of wood.
Director may be the leader and knock other rhythms, or may select student leaders.

Knock, Knock!

Kum bachur atzel
(Hear the Rooster Crowing)

Folk Song from Israel
English Words by David ben Avraham

Kum ba - chur a - tzel___ v' - tzei la - a - vo - da,
Hear the roost - er crow-ing, A - crow - ing at the dawn;

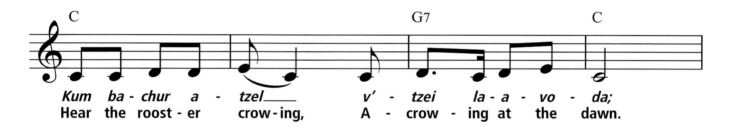

Kum ba - chur a - tzel___ v' - tzei la - a - vo - da;
Hear the roost - er crow-ing, A - crow - ing at the dawn.

Kum, kum,___ v' - tzei la - a - vo - da,
Wake, wake,___ for now the night has gone;

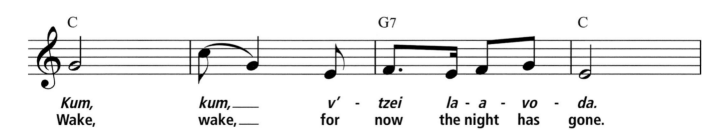

Kum, kum,___ v' - tzei la - a - vo - da.
Wake, wake,___ for now the night has gone.

Kum bachur atzel

Ku - ku - ri - ku,   ku - ku - ri - ku,   tar - n'- gol   ka - ra;

Ku - ku - ri - ku,   ku - ku - ri - ku,   yawn   a might - y   yawn;

Ku - ku - ri - ku,   ku - ku - ri - ku,   tar - n'- gol   ka - ra.

Ku - ku - ri - ku,   ku - ku - ri - ku,   yawn   a might - y   yawn.

La mar estaba serena
(The Sea Is Calm)

Folk Song from Spain
English Words by Bob Demmert

La mar es- ta- ba se- re- na,
The sea is peace-ful and calm now,

se- re- na es- ta- ba la mar.
the sea is qui-et and still.

La mar es- ta- ba se- re- na,
The sea is peace-ful and calm___ now,

se- re- na es- ta- ba la mar.
the sea is qui-et and still.

La víbora
(The Serpent)

Folk Song from Mexico
English Words by Aura Kontra

VERSE

1. Ví - bo - ra, ví - bo - ra, de la mar,
1. Ser - pent,__ ser - pent__ in the sea,
2. O - cho__ ni - ñas__ pa - sa - rán,
2. First one in line will__ run straight through.

por a - quí van a pa - sar,
Soon you'll have some com - pan - y,
o - cho ni - ñas de Tux - pán,
Last one to get here stays with you.

La víbora

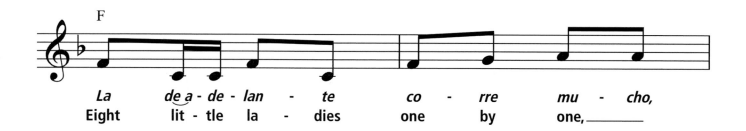

La de a-de-lan-te co-rre mu-cho,
Eight lit-tle la-dies one by one,_____

la de a-trás se que-da-rá.
Eight lit-tle la-dies from Tux-pán.

REFRAIN

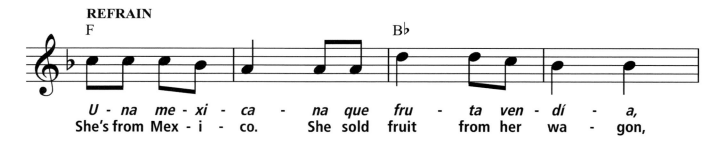

U-na me-xi-ca-na que fru-ta ven-dí-a,
She's from Mex-i-co. She sold fruit from her wa-gon,

Pe-ras, cha-ba-ca-nos, na-ran-jas, san-dí-a.
Or-ang-es and pears, ap-ri-cots, juic-y mel-on.

Leatherwing Bat

Folk Song from the British Isles

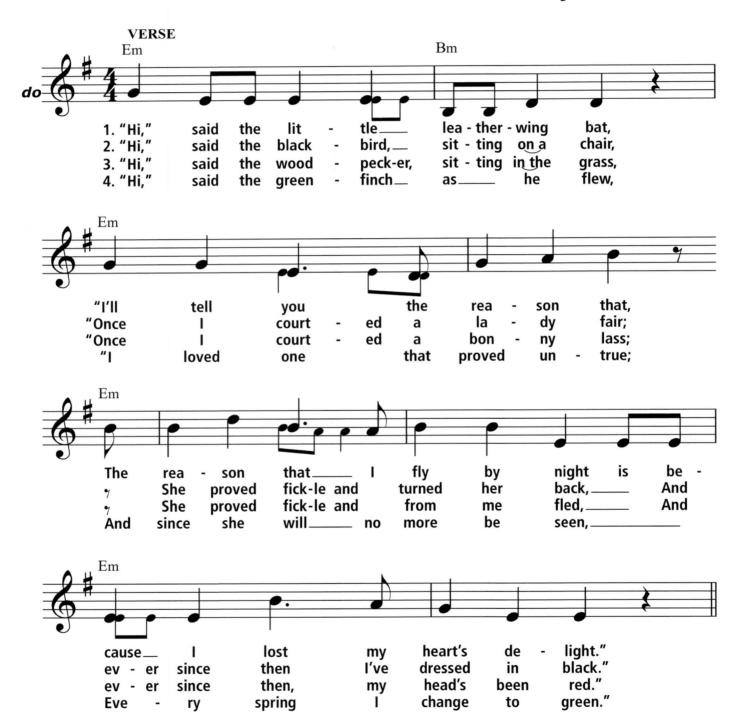

Leatherwing Bat

REFRAIN

How - dy, dow - dy did - dle - o - day,

How - dy, dow - dy did - dle - o - day,

How - dy, dow - dy did - dle - o - day,

How - dy, dow - dy did - dle - o - day.

Lone Star Trail

Cowboy Song from the United States

VERSE

1. I start-ed on the trail on June twen-ty - third,
2. I'm up___ in the mornin' be - fore day - light,
3. Oh, it's ba - con and___ beans 'most ev - 'ry___ day,
4. My feet are in the stirrups and my rope is on the side,

I been punch-in' Tex - as cat - tle on the Lone Star Trail;
And be - fore___ I___ sleep the___ moon shines bright.
I'd as soon___ be a - eat - in'___ prai - rie hay.
Show___ me a horse that___ I can't ride.

REFRAIN

Sing - in' ki yi yip - pi yip - pi yay, yip - pi yay!

Sing - in' ki yi yip - pi yip - pi yay!___

Miss Mary Mack

African American Clapping Game Song

do

G

1. Miss Ma - ry Mack, Mack, Mack,
2. She asked her moth - er, moth - er, moth - er,
3. They jumped so high, high, high,

G

All dressed in black, black, black,
For fif - teen cents, cents, cents,
They touched the sky, sky, sky,

G

With sil - ver but - tons, but - tons, but - tons,
To see the el - e - phants, el - e - phants, el - e - phants
And nev - er came down, down, down,

G

All down her back, back, back.
Jump o - ver the fence, fence, fence.
'Til the fourth of Ju - ly, 'ly, 'ly.

A Mud Puddle Jumped on Me

Words and Music by Carmino Ravosa

My Foot's in My Stirrup

Folk Song from Tennessee
By Louise Bradford

1. My foot's in my stir - rup,
2. I'm go - ing to Geor - gia,
3. Go build me a ca - bin

My reins in my hand,
I'm go - ing to Rome,
on the moun - tain so high

I'm goin' a - way to leave you
I'm go - ing to leave Geor - gia
Where the wild birds and tur - tle dove

for some far dis - tant land.
to make it my home.
can hear my sad cry.

Naranja dulce
(Sweet Orange)

Latin American Singing Game
(Mexico and Costa Rica)
English Words by Eva Laurinda

1. Na - ran - ja dul - ce, li - món par - ti - do,
2. Si fue - ran fal - sos mis ju - ra - men - tos,
1. Sweet hon - ey or - ange, a slice of le - mon,
2. It's time to shake hands, true friends are faith - ful,

da - me un a - bra - zo que yo te pi - do.
en o - tros tiem - pos se ol - vi - dar - an.
give me a hug now, my friend, I'll miss you.
I'll not for - get you, I wish you well._____

3. *Toca la marcha, mi pecho llora,*
   adiós señora, yo ya me voy.

3. The march is playing, it's time to go now,
   Goodbye, my dear friend, I'm sad to leave you.

Old Brass Wagon

Play-Party from the United States

do

G

1. Cir - cle   to   the   left,   old   brass   wag - on;
2. Cir - cle   to   the   right,
3. Swing,   oh,   swing,
4. Prom-e - nade   right,

D   G

Cir - cle   to   the   left,   old   brass   wag - on;
Cir - cle   to   the   right,
Swing,   oh,   swing,
Prom-e - nade   right,

G   A

Cir - cle   to   the   left,   old   brass   wag - on;
Cir - cle   to   the   right,
Swing,   oh,   swing,
Prom-e - nade   right,

D7   C   G

You're   the   one,   my   dar - lin'.

5. Walk it up and down, old brass wagon;
Walk it up and down, old brass wagon;
Walk it up and down, old brass wagon;
You're the one, my darlin'.

6. Break and swing, old brass wagon;
Break and swing, old brass wagon;
Break and swing, old brass wagon;
You're the one, my darlin'.

71

Old Texas

Cowboy Song from Oklahoma

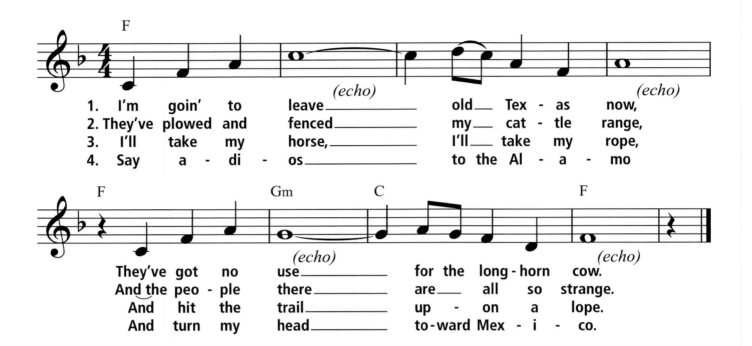

(echo)   *(echo)*

1. I'm goin' to leave_____ old__ Tex - as now,
2. They've plowed and fenced_____ my__ cat - tle range,
3. I'll take my horse,_____ I'll__ take my rope,
4. Say a - di - os_____ to the Al - a - mo

(echo)   *(echo)*

They've got no use_____ for the long - horn cow.
And the peo - ple there_____ are__ all so strange.
And hit the trail_____ up - on a lope.
And turn my head_____ to - ward Mex - i - co.

Olé

Words and Music by
Sally K. Albrecht and Jay Althouse

O - lé,*___ (O - lé,)___ o - lé.___

(o - lé.)___ That's what___ (That's what)

I say.___ All to-geth-er now. O - lé,___

(O - lé,)___ o - lé.___ (o - lé.)___

On the cas - ta-nets, (On the cas - ta-nets,) on the cas - ta-nets

* *Olé* (oh-LAY) – A Spanish word used to express excited approval.

Olé

(on the cas - ta-nets) I will play. (I will play.)

1.

All to - geth - er now.

2.

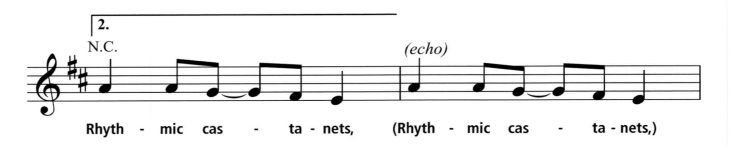

Rhyth - mic cas - ta - nets, (Rhyth - mic cas - ta - nets,)

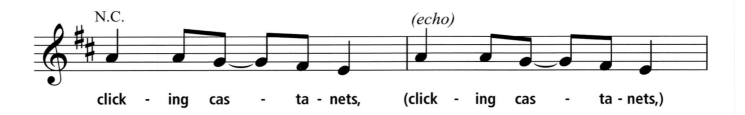

click - ing cas - ta - nets, (click - ing cas - ta - nets,)

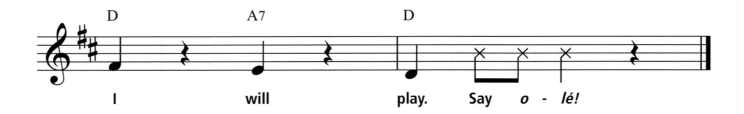

I will play. Say *o - lé!*

Paw-Paw Patch

Play-Party Song from the United States

Allegro

1. Where, O where, is pret-ty lit-tle Su - sie?
2. Come on, boys, let's go find her,
3. Pickin' up paw - paws, put 'em in her pock - ets,

Where, O where, is pret-ty lit-tle Su - sie?
Come on, boys, let's go find her,
Pickin' up paw - paws, put 'em in her pock - ets,

Where, O where, is pret-ty lit-tle Su - sie?
Come on, boys, let's go find her,
Pickin' up paw - paws, put 'em in her pock - ets,

'Way down yon - der in the paw - paw patch.

Pin Pon

Folk Song from Latin America
as sung by Maria de Leon Arcila
English Words by Sue Ellen LaBelle

do–

1. Pin Pon es un mu - ñe - co muy gua - po de car - tón.
2. Cuan - do to - ma la so - pa no en - su - cia el de - lan - tal,
1. Pin Pon's my lit - tle pup - pet, He's hand-some and he's good;
2. Pin Pon joins me for din - ner; he is a wel-come guest;

Se la - va la ca - ri - ta con a - gua y con ja - bón.
Pues co - me con cui - da - do pa - re - ce un ge - ne - ral.
He us - es soap and wa - ter to wash just as he should.
He sips his soup so nice - ly and does - n't make a mess.

Se de - sen - re - da el pe - lo con pie - ne de mar - fil
Y cuan - do las es - tre - llas em - pie - zan a bri - llar,
He has a brush and comb just to make his hair look neat.
When night-time comes up - on us and stars are twink-ling bright,

Y si se da es - ti - ro - nes no llo - ra ni ha - ce a - sí.
Pin Pon se va a la ca - ma se a cues-ta a des - can - sar.
And if he pulls it hard, he still does - n't make a peep.
Pin Pon gets in his bed and I hear him say "Good night."

Popcorn Popping

Music by Betty Lou Cooney
Words by Georgia W. Bello

I looked out the win - dow and what did I see?

Pop - corn pop - ping on the ap - ri - cot tree!

Spring had brought me such a nice sur - prise

Blos - soms pop - ping right be - fore my eyes.

I could take an arm - ful and make a treat,

A pop - corn ball that would smell so sweet. It was - n't real - ly so,

but it seemed to be Pop - corn pop - ping on the ap - ri - cot tree.

Precipitation Day

*Words and Music by
Andy Beck and Brian Fisher*

do —

1. Get out__ your um - brel - la,   it's gon - na rain to - day.
2. Get out__ your to - bog - gan,   it's gon - na snow to - day.

Your slick - er in   yel - la,   the rain is   on the way.
A hat__ for your nog - gin,   the snow is   on the way.

The clouds in   the   heav - ens   are read - y to   go.
The tem - p'ra - ture's fall - ing,   it's go - ing to freeze.

The wa - ter in - side them   is   gon - na o - ver - flow.
Ther - mom - e - ter call - ing, "it's thir - ty - two de - grees."

Precipitation Day

Get out__ your um - brel - la, it's gon - na rain to - day.
Get out__ your to - bog - gan, it's

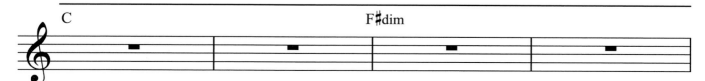

ANCHOR: But wait, the latest weather update predicts a sudden drop in the temperature.

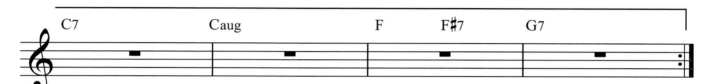

What happens if the air becomes too cold for rain to fall? What will the weather do then?

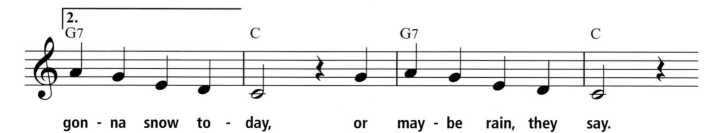

gon - na snow to - day, or may - be rain, they say.

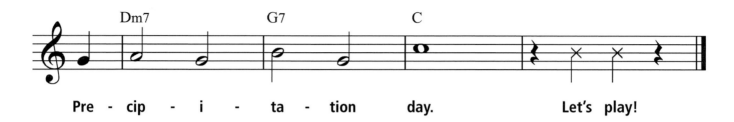

Pre - cip - i - ta - tion day. Let's play!

The Recycle Rap

Words and Music by
Sally K. Albrecht and Jay Althouse

The Recycle Rap

don't for - get the cans, you can crush them when you're through!
try to pay with e - bills. I think you get the gist!

You can see we have a plan.___ Re - cy - cle ev - 'ry - thing you can._

{ Re - use wrap - ping pa - per, rib - bons, ties, and bows. You
{ Look what you are buy - ing, check the pack - ag - ing. If

got - ta love those hand - me - down shoes and hats and clothes.} Re -
it can be re - cy - cled, then that means ev - 'ry - thing. } Re -

1.

cy - cle! It makes you feel so good.

2.

good. It makes you feel so good.

It makes you feel so good. Re - cy - cle!

Riddle Ree

Words and Rhythmic Setting
by Grace Nash

Rocky Mountain

Folk Song from the Southern United States

VERSE

1. Rock - y moun-tain, rock - y moun-tain, rock - y moun-tain high;
2. Sun - ny val - ley, sun - ny val - ley, sun - ny val - ley low;
3. Storm - y o - cean, storm - y o - cean, storm - y o - cean wide;

When you're on that rock - y moun-tain, hang your head and cry!
When you're in that sun - ny val - ley, Sing it soft and slow.
When you're on that deep blue sea, There's no place you can hide.

REFRAIN

Do, do, do, do, Do re - mem - ber me;

Do, do, do, do, Do re - mem - ber me.

Sawatdee tuh jah
(The Hello Song)

Folk Song from Thailand
Collected by Mary Shamrock

Sah - wat - dee   tuh   jah___   rao   mahn   paup   gun,
When we   meet   each   oth - er,   we   say   hel - lo.

Tu   re   chahn___   paup   gun   sah - wat - dee.
When   we   meet, ___   we   say   hel - lo.

Shake My Maracas

Words and Music by
Sally K. Albrecht and Jay Althouse

Oh, come and hear me shake my ma - ra - cas.

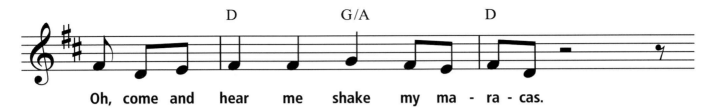

Oh, come and hear me shake my ma - ra - cas.

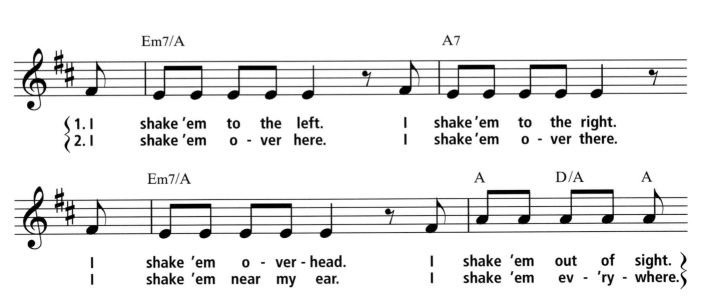

1. I shake 'em to the left. I shake 'em to the right.
2. I shake 'em o - ver here. I shake 'em o - ver there.

I shake 'em o - ver - head. I shake 'em out of sight.
I shake 'em near my ear. I shake 'em ev - 'ry - where.

Shake My Maracas

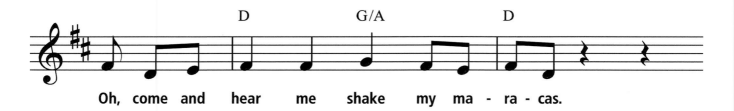

Oh, come and hear me shake my ma - ra - cas.

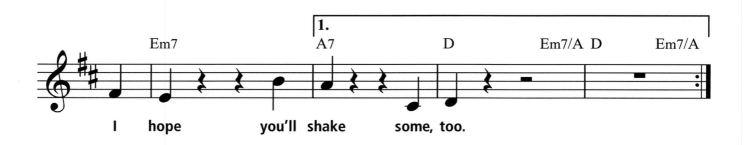

Oh, come and hear me shake my ma - ra - cas.

I hope you'll shake some, too.

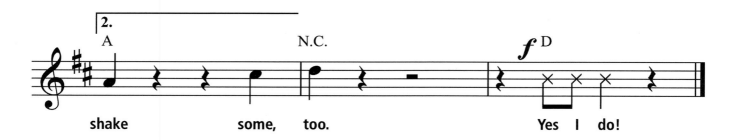

shake some, too. Yes I do!

Shake Them 'Simmons Down

Play-Party Song from Texas

1. Cir - cle right,
2. Cir - cle left,
3. Boys to the cen - ter,
4. Girls to the cen - ter,
do - oh, do - oh,

Cir - cle right,
Cir - cle left,
Boys to the cen - ter,
Girls to the cen - ter,
do - oh, do - oh,

Cir - cle right,
Cir - cle left,
Boys to the cen - ter,
Girls to the cen - ter,
do - oh, do - oh,

Shake them 'sim - mons down.

5. Promenade all, do-oh, do-oh,
   Promenade all, do-oh, do-oh,
   Promenade all, do-oh, do-oh,
   Shake them 'simmons down.

6. Swing your corner, do-oh, do-oh,
   Swing your corner, do-oh, do-oh,
   Swing your corner, do-oh, do-oh,
   Shake them 'simmons down.

She'll Be Comin' 'Round the Mountain

Railroad Song

Shoo, Fly

Folk Song from the United States

Shoo, fly, don't both - er me, Shoo, fly, don't both - er me,

Fine

Shoo, fly, don't both - er me, For I be - long to some - bod - y.

I feel, I feel, I feel, I feel like a morn - ing star,

D.C. al Fine

I feel, I feel, I feel, I feel, I feel like a morn - ing star. So,

Sing a Rainbow

Words and Music by Arthur Hamilton

Sing a Rainbow

Lis - ten with your eyes, lis - ten with your eyes

and sing ev - 'ry - thing you see.

You can sing a rain - bow, sing a rain - bow,

D.C. al Fine

sing a - long with me.

Skinnamarink

Adapted and Arranged
by Michael Story

Skin-na-ma-rink a - dink - a-dink, skin-na-ma-rink a - doo,

I love you.

Skin-na-ma-rink a - dink - a-dink, skin-na-ma-rink a - doo,

I love you.

I love you in the morn-ing___ and in the af-ter-noon,

Skinnamarink

I love you in the eve-ning_____ and un-der-neath the

moon.   Oh,_____   Skin - na - ma - rink   a -

dink - a - dink,   skin - na - ma - rink   a - doo,

I   love   you.

Somebody Waiting

Play-Party Song from the United States

1. As I look in-to your eyes, I be-hold a glad sur-prise,

There is some-bod-y wait-ing for me.

2. There is some-bod-y wait-ing, there is some-bod-y wait-ing,
3. Now choose two, leave the oth-ers, now choose two, leave the oth-ers,
4. Swing the one, leave the oth-er, swing the one, leave the oth-er,

There is some-bod-y wait-ing for me.
Now choose two, leave the oth-ers for me.
Swing the one, leave the oth-er for me.

Thanksgiving Is Near

Words and Music by Grace Nash and Janice Rapley

do–

1. Oc - to - ber is o - ver, Thanks - giv - ing is near.
2. The Thanks - giv - ing ta - ble is load - ed with treats. It's

Can't you smell tur - key and stuff - ing right here?
hard to use cau - tion and not o - ver - eat.

And when it is o - ver and thanks have been said,
But when it is o - ver and I'm stuffed in bed,

it won't be the tur - key but me stuffed in - stead!
I'll wish that the tur - key had gob - bled in - stead.

Tideo

Play-Party Song from Texas

Pass one win-dow Ti - de - o, Pass two win-dows Ti - de - o,

Pass three win-dows Ti - de - o, Jin-gle at the win - dow Ti - de - o.

Ti - de - o, Ti - de - o, Jin-gle at the win - dow Ti - de - o.

Tideo

Rhythm: Reading ♩, ♫, and ♬♬

Waiting for the Traffic Light

Words and Music by David Connors

Swing Style

We're wait-ing for the traf-fic light to turn to green.

If it ev-er hap-pens it re-mains to be seen.__ As we

wait for the light we will start to move.__

We can feel the rhy-thm and get in-to the groove.

Waiting for the Traffic Light

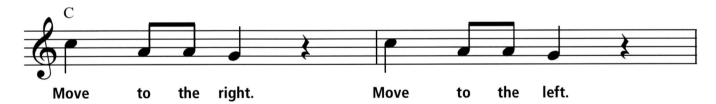

Move to the right. Move to the left.

Move in a way that you like best.___

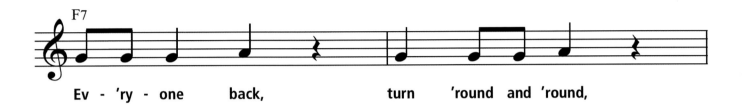

Ev - 'ry - one back, turn 'round and 'round,

Ev - 'ry - one for - ward, touch the ground.

We Wish You a Merry Christmas

Carol from England

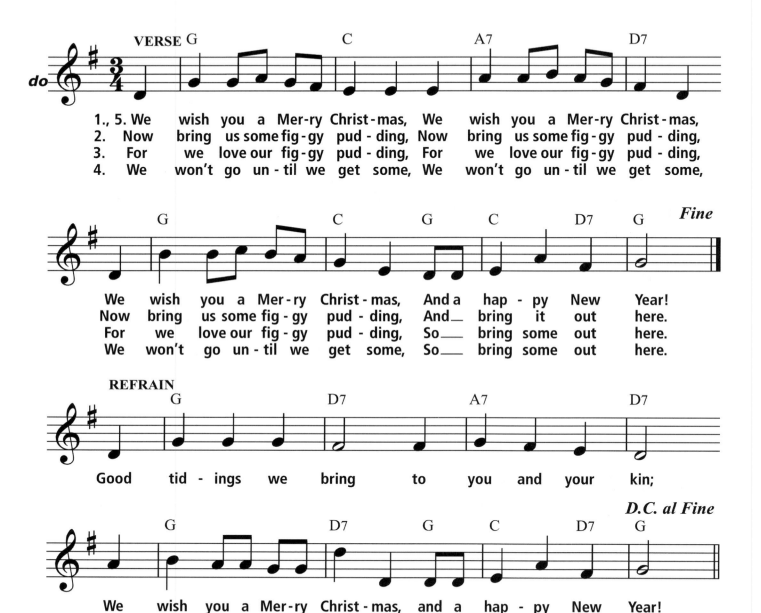

1., 5. We wish you a Mer-ry Christ-mas, We wish you a Mer-ry Christ-mas,
2. Now bring us some fig-gy pud-ding, Now bring us some fig-gy pud-ding,
3. For we love our fig-gy pud-ding, For we love our fig-gy pud-ding,
4. We won't go un-til we get some, We won't go un-til we get some,

We wish you a Mer-ry Christ-mas, And a hap-py New Year!
Now bring us some fig-gy pud-ding, And__ bring it out here.
For we love our fig-gy pud-ding, So__ bring some out here.
We won't go un-til we get some, So__ bring some out here.

REFRAIN

Good tid-ings we bring to you and your kin;

We wish you a Mer-ry Christ-mas, and a hap-py New Year!

Who Has Seen the Wind?

Melody from Zion's Harp
Words by Christina Rossetti

Xiao yin chuan
(Silver Moon Boat)

Folk Song from China

Yue er wan wan xiang yi tiao chuan gua tian shang
Lit - tle sil - ver moon rides the sky like a boat,

Chuan guo xing xing ta yi ran qing ying piao dang
Past the twink-ling stars it will float, light - ly float.

Yang fan___ xiang zhe xi fang hang
Sail, lit - tle moon boat, to the west,

Jia xiao xiao yin chuan duo an xiang.
Sail, lit - tle moon boat, while I rest.

Xiao yin chuan
(Silver Moon Boat)

Rhythm: Reading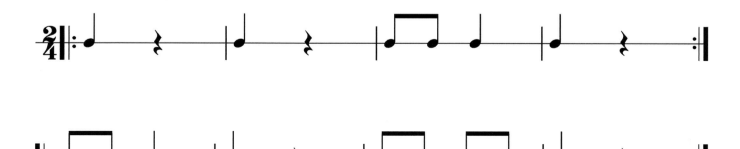

Zudio

Traditional Street Song from the United States

Zudio

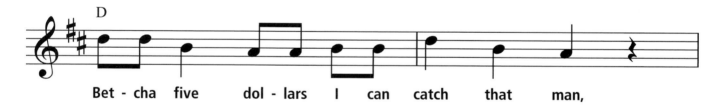

Bet - cha five dol - lars I can catch that man,

Bet - cha five dol - lars I can catch that man. To the

side, to the side, to the side, side, side; To the

side, to the side, to the side, side, side,

Side, side, side. My

Zudio

ma - ma called the doc - tor; the doc - tor said, ___

"Oo, oh, ___ I got a pain in my head." To the
"Oo, oh, ___ I got a pain in my tum."
"Oo, oh, ___ I got a pain in my side."

side, to the side, to the side, side, side; ___ To the

side, to the side, to the side, side, side, ___ Side, side, side. ___